The Owning Stone

The Owning Stone

poems by

Jim Peterson

RED HEN PRESS | *Pasadena, CA*

The Owning Stone
Copyright © 2000 by Jim Peterson
Second Edition 2011

All rights reserved

No part of this book may be used or reproduced in any manner whatsoever without the prior written permission of both the publisher and the copyright owner.

Book design and layout by Kathrine Davidson
Cover art adapted from "The Lamp"
Color woodblock print by John Buck

ISBN: 978-1-59709-491-7
Library of Congress Catalog Card Number: 00-192043

The Los Angeles County Arts Commission, the California Arts Council, the National Endowment for the Arts, and City of Los Angeles Department of Cultural Affairs partially support Red Hen Press.

Published by Red Hen Press
www.redhen.org

Acknowledgments

Grateful acknowledgment is made to the editors of the following journals in which these poems first appeared: *Akros Review*: "Uncle"; *Ascent*: "Privacy"; *Chariton Review*: "The Motel," "Let Me Find It"; *Cincinnati Poetry Review*: "The Messengers"; *Connecticut Review*: "The Crawl"; *Clockwatch Review*: "Daughter"; *Georgia Review*: "Something," "Opening Night," "Fish to Fry," "The Part About Guns," "The Owning Stone"; *Greensboro Review*: "The Guest"; *Interim*: "One by One," "Finesse"; *Kennesaw Review*: "The Chair"; *Kestrel*: "Before Daylight"; *King Log*: "Something Old"; *Laurel Review*: "Not the One," "Remission," "The Men," "Sculptor," "The Seeds of Unkindness"; *One Meadway*: "The View From Above"; *Poetry*: "The Other"; *Poetry Northwest*: "Someone's Father," "My Mother's Back," "Why you Must Have a Motorcycle"; *Prairie Schooner*: "Not talking at Dawn," "Mantis"; *Snail's Pace Review*: "A Drawing of the Laughing Jesus"; *Southern Poetry Review*: "Paid Vacation"; *Tar River Poetry*: "Now Leasing," "The Man in the Green Truck"; *Texas Review*: "King Queen Jack"; and in a limited edition chapbook *Carvings on a Prayer Tree* (Holocene Press, 1994): "The Other."

For Harriet

*and for my mother, Jewelle,
and my sisters, Patti and Gayle,
and in memory of my father, James,*

*and with much gratitude to the many poet-friends and editors who read all
or part of this manuscript and offered helpful comments:
Claire Bateman, Warren Slesinger, Pattiann Rogers, Peter Meinke, Tami
Haaland, Randall Gloege, Donna Davis, Anna Elkins, David Starkey,
Cecile Goding, Steve Gardner, and most especially Rebecca McClanahan
and Steve Corey,*

*and with much gratitude to the editors of my first two books,
Warren Slesinger of The Bench Press and John Lane of Holocene Press
for believing in my poems.*

Contents

The Owning Stone   13

Someone's Father

Something Old	19
Someone's Father	20
Daughter	22
Fish to Fry	24
The View From Above	25
Remission	28
Play Ball	32
Trucks and All	34
The Part About Guns	36
My Mother's Back	38

Not Talking

Sculptor	43
Now Leasing	46
King Queen Jack	48
Why You Must Have a Motorcycle	52
Not the One	54
The Seeds of Unkindness	56
Mantis	58
The Men	61
The Man in the Green Truck	66

The Chair	68
Not Talking At Dawn	70
The Crawl	72

Let Me Find It

The Other	75
The Motel	78
One by One	80
Opening Night	82
Something	84
A Drawing of the Laughing Jesus	86
Paid Vacation	88
Finesse	90
The Messengers	92
Privacy	94
The Guest	96
Before Daylight	98
Uncle	100
Let Me Find It	102

The Owning Stone

The Owning Stone

1. *The Ritual*

Three years ago I cleared this field
dragged the pines and sweetgums
and stacked them at the edge
home now for black widows and hog-nosed snakes
and the green-turning-to-brown chameleons
I left three great oaks and half a dozen dogwoods
scattered the bahia seed by hand and now
the grass is good enough for grazing
but there will be no horses here nor cows
I say to the oaks
this stone has traveled one thousand miles
from the edge of cliffs and salt water
I chose it for its size and weight
for the way it lies in the palm
for the way it both absorbs and reflects the light
but trees already know the heft of stones
hold them in their roots for a hundred years
so I throw the stone to a far corner and run
to find it burrowing under dead leaves
I throw it again to another corner and another
then into the center then out again to the edge
running to find it each time
making these trees this grass this piece of land my own

2. *Voices*

Last night I named the stone
when it was too tired to be thrown
and when it refused to take the light
from my lamp into its crystal striation
in the silence of these old walls the stone
reminded me of my father's sightless
eye that looked both dead and alive at once
William of the dapper wingtips

and the big plans that sometimes worked
of the two day beard on weekends
and the smell of hard sleep that lingered on his body
of the tiny voice that leaked from his bad eye
when he dozed in the summer dusk

while I lay close against him and that small
voice like the TV turned very low said
stay right where you are kid and you'll succeed
and I said *I'm going to live far away in Texas
or Maine where the lobsters are free and the cliffs
are like castles looming over the stormy ocean*
and the eye just laughed and rolled aimlessly
in my father's head

3. *Mirth*

I want to speak to the stone
but I know it will only listen
named for the eye of a dead man
it is a blurred face in the background of a photo
less than that
less than something lost and forgotten
nothing without me
the object of a game of solitaire
cold in my hand empty of everything
but itself and I open the door and hurl it
its flight invisible in the darkness
the tree frogs are full of mirth
the whippoorwills are voices within voices
the stone drops onto soft ground far away
and creeps under leaves

4. *Choice*

I can imagine the flight of anything
especially a stone named
William who was my father and who owned everything
one thousand throws of a stone in every direction
it could not hide from me in the dawn
I would take the stone back to where I found it

but the price of a ticket is high and the car is blowing smoke
I would throw it in the lake
but I know I would only follow it
and its advantages in deep water are great

no I must own up to the fact of this stone
I have chosen it and it me though it complains bitterly
it is my one simplicity my one secret
true because no one wants it
what remains of my father's land can hold it

here you can take it for a while
let it ride among your change let it ride
in your breast pocket among the points of pens
let it become lost among your papers
or under the furniture of an unused room
and I will find it some night when we
have talked ourselves into morning
as I first found it one day in July
on the coast of Maine in a small cove
where the grains of sand were stones

Someone's Father

Something Old

hand in hand with my son and father
I walk through grass so dark in its greenness
it darkens the sky
we play follow the leader
we hang from a limb
scratching and snarfing
we roll in the grass cultivating an itch
we throw out our voices
they turn in the distance over trees
and tumble back to us
full of the coolness of wind and rain
at night we build a fire
the flash of blade-light
over the shins of trees
the small faces of leaves

Someone's Father

on a business trip to a city
not so different from my own
I discovered a child
she was laughing and running
along the paths under an old bridge
in the late afternoon shadows
I stood among her footprints and she found me
grabbing at my empty hand
as if I could be someone's father
who knew where the painted egg lay in high grass
who spoke in secret whispers that brought
the dog forth from under the porch
who created with a wave of his hand
the empty day
I was just tired
just looking for a grassy bank to lie down
but she had me now this small wild person
leading me by the hand in wavy circles
to a clump of weeds to a big rock
to a place where wind moved grains of sand
she made me get down on my knees
and wait till I saw it for myself
and she was singing little bits of songs
in her careless voice
a bird addressing its own shadow in the leaves
leaning all forty of her pounds
to lug me along to a crack in the sidewalk
where tiny ants traveled safe and unseen
to a garbage can where drunken bees

lay curled up in the sun
see she said they're sleeping
to the corner of a house where water dripped
from the roof
and made a bright green patch
to a front door swung wide open
and three empty rooms smelling of lysol
clean rooms the light shining on floors
the windows open and a breeze blowing through
and this little girl running back and forth
in the straightest line she knew
with both hands raised
helping the air to find its way across

Daughter

He hasn't heard a word she's said.

After ten hours at the plant
he stands in the front yard and stares
into the tops of red maples and sweetgums,
absently watering the lawn and shrubs.

Clouds glow red at the edges
like coals in a breeze.
She curls her toes in the mud,
feels herself growing,
stretches her thin arms
above her head, sees herself
as a tree, rooted, blown by the wind.

The water unwinds from his hand,
carves the dark ground at her feet.
The tops of his maples sway
like the veiled faces of women.

Suddenly cold, she goes inside,
watches him through windows,
immobile, only the water moving,
and the trees. The red tint of clouds
turns gray, then black. The house
grows dark in every room.

In darkness he sees the wind,
knows the trees are touching

each other deep underground
where the voices begin and end,
surfacing in the mouths of children.
Remembers the way his wife's
brown hair fanned on the pillow,
the way he touched it and the hot
curve of her throat. He lets the hose

fall, wagging in the slick grass.
His hands reach out, encircle
the cold rough waist of a sweetgum.
He sees her asleep among roots,
dreaming of evergreens, wild grass.

His daughter goes to bed hungry,
window open, breeze sliding over her
like the hands of ghosts.
She asked him once about love and men,
but he just folded his arms, shook
his head over and over, eyes
not looking out at her, but in
at something only he could see.

All night she hears the water.
It floods the yard and garden
beneath her window,
slowly climbing the wall.

Fish to Fry

An unsolved murder, a flock of thieves
circling the city among pigeons, a bomb
threat and the real thing raining debris
into the streets, these are the fish fried
in the same pan day after day. And if
the young girl escapes the rapist's grasp,
plunging into the shocked headlights
of a busy road, her story is thrown
back into the pond of her own dreams,
a shark lurking among the bass and bream.
But if she disappears for days, if her
body is found in the woods, every drop
of the spirit squeezed out of her like
water from a new sponge, flash-bulbs
sprout up around her like magic tulips,
voices crawl into her wounds like insects,
the hands of white-coated men break her
further open like so much suspicious fruit.
It is the clues they want, the innuendoes
of brutality, of the final bursting into
flames of her desire to live. Next day,
we will feed upon her as the killer fed,
our eyes moving from column to column
like the wild boar's snout over ground.
By afternoon, her story will be fit
kindling for the evening fire, fit
wrapping for the last lucky catch at dusk.

The View From Above

This is before color came,
when there were Sundays.

In the basement bedroom,
windows look out at ground level
over lawn and surface roots of trees.

My father is slowly waking
and I am still and small beside him.
His head emerges from pillows,
hair swept into a stationary storm,
hot body smelling of sleep.

Waiting for the battle of Redskins and Colts,
we watch the black and white
flickering to us, live,
the miracles of a man on stage
in a great tent that holds thousands
who raise their hands or stand
to shout "Amen" at his command.
Black tie loosened,
gray coat thrown across a chair,
white sleeves rolled for work,
he takes each head
at first in his huge hands,
crazed hope
surfacing in each face
from the force of his twisting grip,
the jerk that surges

healing power: goiters
shrink and disappear,
crutches wave like stripped wings
as the lame walk haltingly
to hallelujahs down the ramp.

Twenty years later
at the end of a long flight,
we meet with that man
at his University of Faith
in color now, a golfer's
green and blue and tan.

In a sanctum of his Citadel of Prayer
he tells my father
to square his life with everyone
and to turn his face toward God.
Then he takes the nape
of my father's neck
in his hot right hand
and commands the marrow of my father's bones
to behave itself.
Before we leave
he gives us signed copies
of his book on faith.

On the plane going home
for a change we see nothing but each other,
hear nothing but our own voices
full of the forgiving words
we could never say before.
We speak of our dreams,
of the blood cells raging in his body
like the tiny scrambling dots that are cars
on the freeway beneath us
cutting through the patterned fields of farms,
the diminishing patches of woods.
He says he's afraid.
We pass through the white mist of clouds
as if it were nothing.

Remission

In the last year of his life
my father walks
along this blind-curving path,
pauses for a moment
to watch the crows leap and call
among the high limbs of poplars.
He hunted them for sport
when he was a boy, pests
to the farmers,
to the back-yard gardeners.
He sees the light gather
under their outstretched wings,
hears for the first time
an answering silence
between their calls.

On an afternoon in 1955
my nightmares coalesced
in the eyes of an old black man
driving his horse and wagon
up the paved road behind our house,
shovels and rakes rattling in the bed.
I dove into the underbrush
of a patch of woods and listened
to the chinking of metal tack,
the out-of-round wheels
creaking and grinding,
watched the giant man
and the giant horse,

white foam dripping
from its whiskered lips,
the old man's hands
shining in the sun
like the wings of crows,
snapping the reins gently
against the flanks of the horse
that never changed its steady walk
or its cloudy, contented gaze.
But the old man had seen me,
pulled to a halt,
stared into the swirl of thorns
and thwarted scrub oaks
where I lay trying not to breathe
against the gray leaves.
"You all right boy?" The horse
stamped its foot. The old man
leaned and maneuvered his head.
"What you afraid of?"

One night in 1964
my father could not shake
the words of a speech by Malcolm X.
He sat on the edge of his bed,
boxer shorts gaping open,
reading-glasses at the tip of his nose.
He cracked his pistol open,
spun the empty cylinder,
clicked the .32's into chambers,

snapped it back together
with a flick of his wrist.
There had been riots
in the streets of Augusta,
blacks shot in the back as they ran,
whites pulled from their cars and beaten,
the old stores of Broad Street
set to flame. At dawn,
the birds outside my father's window
would not shut up.
Propping his elbow on the sill,
he sighted them one at a time
down the short, polished barrel of his gun.

Sometimes at night
my father and I faced each other
over bowls of cereal
and argued long past the eating
until neither one of us could sleep.
Finally, one night
in the summer of 1967,
he admitted that King
was a good man, then
squawked his dinette chair
back from the table
and raised his hand
like a preacher in benediction
to stop my words.
He balled his hand into a fist.

His head trembled.
"But he wants too much," he said,
and left the room.

In the Spring of 1977,
in the last remission
of my father's long dying,
we watch the crows
cavorting in the overreaching trees.
Where are the robins and the wrens?
But he loves the crows, the way
they shake the whole tree.
I climb into my car to leave,
and how quickly my father turns away.
He stands in the yard,
the grass still brown from winter,
the last rays of sun raking
the tops of trees.
He raises his hands from his sides
and his face to the sky streaked with cirrus.
The crows come from everywhere,
and the heads of pines
grow dark and heavy and alive.

Play Ball

My friend and I were never

the slugs when we were kids;
we pitied them. We commanded
the river of ants that surrounded them.
We rode astride the great necks of beetles
forcing the grass to part before us,
such zealous stealth among the stems.

And what terrible crossings
under the sun, taking refuge
in the reflective coolness of centerlines.
The slugs were kings overthrown
by ungrateful hordes, forced
in their escape to wear those
glistening capes of disguise.

"What are you boys doing out there?"
my friend's mother would yell
from the porch. Later on his father
would want to know what was so
damned interesting about dirt and bugs.
He played catch with a hard rubber ball
against the garage. He laid three leather

gloves, a real baseball, and a Louisville
Slugger on the grass. Before crawling
out to join him we hunkered out of sight
among the roots of a huge oak, staring up
into the arched cloud of its canopy,
wondering what the journey would be like,
that long climb into flickering light.

Trucks and All

This is where I found
a small boy playing with his trucks.
Because it's such a lonely place
and he was so lost in his game,
I didn't know how to approach
without frightening him.
I whistled loudly,
stopped to inspect a mushroom,
to give him time to adjust.
I have no children
and I wanted to steal him,
trucks and all. Instead,
I stepped wide of him into mud
and ruined my shoes. Looking back,
I saw that he hadn't noticed me,
those tiny hands maneuvering dump trucks,
building roads and bridges.
That night I dreamed of the boy,
the way those engines rumbled in his throat,
the way the voices of his drivers
shouted to each other
to get the job done.
Next day in my office,
I propped my feet on the desk.
Dried mud fell onto contracts,
and I remembered playing
with my father's shoes,
dump trucks across the living room floor
with their loads of marbles and paper clips,

roadsters that carried men to their offices.
There was much I could pass on to this boy.
After work I walked down the same
isolated path in the park,
the patch of mud filled-in with soft dirt.
The tracks of tiny wheels
crisscrossed everywhere, disappearing
into raised oak-roots and underbrush.

The Part About Guns

there was a man who dreamed of guns
he had never owned a gun
never held one in his hand
never cracked a pistol open
and spun the cylinder
had never clicked .38's into their caves

this was a man who hated guns
he would not watch movies with guns
TV programs with guns
he would not allow one into his house
no matter how shiny the steel
how nifty the weight in his hand

when a gun came to his door
he was polite but firm
it did not matter that its chambers were empty
that its butt was presented first
that the safety was on
and the trigger had no play

he refused to sight down the barrel
to enjoy the smell of gun oil
to cup the handle in his palm
to slide his finger through the trigger loop
but his dreams persisted
so he stayed awake

he tried to read but laid the book down
when it got to the part about guns
the books stacked up like piles of hands
under the hanging lamp of his kitchen table
beside his lounge chair in the living room
beside his bed

and when he fell asleep in spite of himself
the guns of women's feet
discharged in the street
the gun of his own dog's head
defended the yard against children
their bloodless bodies

like broken loaves of bread in the grass
the guns of his father's hands
clapped in the den
and the voice said dance
and he danced and danced all night
his toes barely touching the floor

My Mother's Back

I had failed for months to see my mother.
I was far away, I reasoned. Now she was
maimed by this pain, by this knot of cancer
curled around her spine.

To see the crow on the low limb
not ten feet from my face,
I was surprised I did not have to dance barefoot
all day on burning stones.

A steer stood nearby in the hot ravine.
It leaned among rock shadows,
stirred the dust with a split hoof
and stared at me with amazed eyes.

This was no time of meditation,
of sinking into reverie. Not even
the clarity of wanting nothing. Not even
the peace of wanting something so simple

as finding the familiar track of a mule deer
in sand. The crow's feet scraped bark.
He cocked his head and glared at everything
but me. Such blackness was an edgy

absence among the leaves. The wind
curved over him like water over stones.
The rock face behind him caught the sun
and swelled into copper and gold.

But still he did not fly. Nor did I,
sitting plank-backed among the rocks,
trying not to think at all, not to find her face
in the shadows shuffling over the canyon wall.

Not Talking

Sculptor

the man has been patient for days
watching this stone fold
and unfold its shadow like a map

the stone says *listen*
I want to wait in a bus station
Reds cap pulled down low
duffle bag full of stale clothes
want to ride into the city and walk
under the obscene lights
where even the pigeons
stay up all night on the ledges
want to rent a cheap room
where the faucet drips on a rusty stain
where roaches hang from the walls like fruit bats
I want to raise the window
prop it open with an old Bible
listen to the crying and laughing
on the street below
I want to dial a number
then wait with lights off
for the sound of steps in the hall

the man is bored with this stone
thinks about walking into woods
where twisted limbs suggest possibilities
but the stone says *listen*
I want to eat a club sandwich toothpicks and all
want to work behind counters

touching the customers' hands as I make change
want to stretch out on the floor and count the cracks
lighting one cigarette off another
till I fill the room
want to walk out into rain
and stand with old men huddled under awnings
and share my own stories of the underground
want to wear a tuxedo and hover
over the jewelled cleavage of women
want to comb my hair while pissing
into the scented urinal
then find my face in the mirror
and stare into my own curious eyes

the man is disgusted
imagines instead a lone figure in a field
slender as an egret
graceful as a sweep of cirrus
a small path wandering through pines
and hip-high grass to find it
but the stone says *forget it*
you fat-drinking old farmer
I want to touch the thigh of a woman
and feel her hand say no then yes
I want to sleep then wake up then sleep again
I want to lick my fingers and throw away the bones
the man backs away from the stone
studies its face
can't remember what he'd seen there

the stone says *listen here*
you brain-heavy little mole
but the man is tired
all day he has been drawing
the stone's coldness into his hands
he turns off the lights
listen to me
you sliver-pinching old worm
you root-sucking two-legged bastard
he climbs into bed beside his wife
stone-roughened hand sliding
down the warm length of her body

Now Leasing

The man in the empty space
is busy. Already he has taken down
the great black and white letters.
The clean glass reflects passersby

and cars flash-filling the window's
one instant. He takes his place
among reflections, but when the sunlight
recedes behind buildings, he is the one

remaining. Now shoppers stop to stare
into his dimly lit cave. He cannot
rest with so much to be done. Empty
cans gather in corners, under tables.

Tools trail behind him like the litter of bums.
He stands the nails upright one by one
and drives them. With each white stroke
he denies the dull gray of a former loan office.

He erects the metal shelves, cardboard displays,
presses the ten thousand tiny mouths of pegboard
against the walls. One day trucks arrive
and the tools multiply. He lifts each one

carefully to its assigned place,
checking himself in each shiny surface,
red eyes, thin mouth beginning to curve.
Now the hammers are hung by their claws,

the bubbles of stacked levels centered and still.
The saws are goofy in his hands,
guffawing back to temporary silence.
Nuts and bolts are poured into drawers

according to size and use. The cave swells richly
inward, and the man withdraws behind his counter.
At first, the others gaze in his window,
then stroll through his rows, pausing to feel

the heft of a swingblade, to read the label
on a can of paint. And the man springs from his
corner to guide them to one small purchase
after another. He cannot stop measuring the spaces

he must fill. He cannot stop smiling.

King Queen Jack

    Ask me what I know.
    I know how to trap and kill,
    how to cook meat slow
    over a smokeless fire.
    I know where huckleberries grow,
    where scuppernongs thicken
    over old fence-wire.
    I know a good game of cards.

The way Wally used to tell it
he found me next to dumpsters
on Highway 34, wrapped in wet
newspaper. Some nights I see it too,
how he shook his head,
threw his hands in the air
like he was preaching:
"Idiot God," he said.
How he lifted that bundle
to the seat of his pickup
and pulled a dirty shirt around it.
Then stooped for scrap lumber,
tin cans in the high weeds,
and drove me home to Angela.
Her hair was red and stringy,
eyes bright gray like clouds.
She washed the news from my body,
encircled me on the bed
with her lean arms, and sang
about kings and princes.

Ask me what I know.
I know this blue house
where you cook and clean,
waiting for good news. I know
the way you brush your hair,
the way you lie in the grass
when the others are asleep
and stare at the stars.
Once, I waited until the sun
was whole above the trees,
watched you in your housecoat
pick up the paper
I'd left far out near the curb.
I know the way your eyes met mine.

I used to dream I was born
of a woman instead of old news,
of a man who drove to work.
But I woke to Wally's
crooked grin, the smell
of whiskey and rabbit blood,
Angela's hands over the fire
like huge moths. She pulled
this worn deck from her pocket
wrapped in rubber bands.
"King Queen Jack," she said,
a game she'd made up
for the three of us, her face
like an old rose in the fire-shadows,

speckled hands dealing out
the cards she could read
from either side. She always won.

Ten years like that. I buried
Angie first, Wally three months later,
in the hill behind their shack.

>   I know how to rise wide awake
>   in the pitch black, how to kill
>   a fire and leave no trace.
>   Every dawn, I drive by this house
>   and throw the news
>   onto your sandy patch of grass.
>   I know the smell of your bacon and eggs,
>   how the slanted rays of morning
>   strike your window, warm the colors
>   of the afghan, the bright animal
>   walls of that empty room,
>   the daffodils your husband picks.

I have this dream.
You leave your breakfast half eaten,
kitten scratching on her box,
TV with a face talking and the sound
off, husband in his office,
and walk from lawn into underbrush.
I hear the shuffle of your steps in leaves,
see the yellow flash of your hair,

smell your scent like strawberries.
You run barefoot through the woods,
find a spot where the pinestraw is flat
and the sun breaks through.
You curl up and sleep.

    I know when the signs are right.
    Today, the sky is clear, the street
    empty. Your back door was open.
    It's hard to breathe in here.
    I could watch you all day, asleep
    on this couch. I am waiting for you
    to wake. King Queen Jack,
    I shuffle the deck and deal.

Why You Must Have a Motorcycle

Say you cannot unwind the sheets from your legs,
or ancient trees have fallen across your lawn
and require the chainsaw which you refuse to own,
or five select chairs lined up in a row
cannot make you comfortable, or the street
black and glazed with rainwater is as empty
as you would have it, or yes, the players
come off the field and they are too real,
they are boys or men who wish nothing more
than to spend their lives playing this game
while somewhere there is a fist filling up with rage—

say there is money involved and you must get up
or today there are single words frying on the pan
of your brain and allowing any one of them to rise
into your body into the warm hum of your throat
to pass through your tongue and lips. . . . is to weep,
or maybe yesterday's socks are still fresh enough
and what you know about this day is that it is
happening somewhere else, right?, in some street
full of smoke and waiting, in some ditch, in some
alley, in some room grown small with voice
where the body grows small, the heart, the face—

still you will stare at the walls on which you
have placed the photographs of your mother
and father, your wife and children saying cheese,
your dog standing in a field of flowers gazing
at mountains, or your cats curled together
in the rocking chair, of yourself victorious
on the cliff's precipice next to one large raven
who held his place on a sandstone rock where you
wanted to stand, of the Harley-Davidson
you once owned and drove without a helmet
and sold in a fit of reason, and now wish to own again.

Not the One

when the other children called her dumb
when the other children called her ugly
she broke a limb off the tree
and scratched her wrist and forearm
bearing down with the weight of her body
the dull head digging in
the scream too thick in her throat
to come out
she knows what she's supposed to be

she lives in this village for the mindless
she works each day till she sleeps
she stumbles over the wooden bridge from the laundry
bubbles in her hair
water spots on her slacks
and something in you hides
she lumbers toward you like an old heavyweight
and throws her fists around you
she brings you the animal of her breath
that grapples with your face
she brings you an apple bruised and bitten
she brings you the bloody stick
and the blood among old scars
she brings you her father the mayor
and her mother the cultured woman
who must speak to you in private
she brings you a thousand times more
than you can take
and defeat steps in and pulls her back

the thick roots of her feelings curling up like toes
she turns from the words
she knows you have to say
you try to tell yourself
her tears are not sacred
her blood just the sign of a wound
you tell her that you love her
but so have the others
from her door
she brings out the pails and the water
the cleaners the rags the broom and the mop
she knows that you're just one of the ones
that's not the one

The Seeds of Unkindness

It's a cold day in summer
and a woman I have tried to forget
walks down the sidewalk
in a small town I am only passing through.
I circle the block and park
and watch her shuffle toward me.
I like that word "shuffle"
because it makes her seem stupid.
She wears a man's sweater
many sizes too large
and her hands curl up in the sleeves,
just the knuckles peeking out
like seedlings. I don't like
that word for her,
but that's what I see.
When I was small
and my mother had to work,
this woman slapped me
and knocked me over a chair—
and said if I told she would kill me.
Every day when my mother left for work
I grew small and hard
like the acorns in my grandmother's yard.
I did what I was told,
I kept my hands together and my head down,
so quiet that even this mean woman
with references, Mary, called me strange.
That was a word she liked for me.
She stops beside my window,

pulls used tissue from her pocket,
wipes her upper lip.
I lean across my front seat
to stare at her, ready, finally,
for a fight. But I cannot take my eyes
away from those small white hands
emerging from their sleeves
like hermit crabs.
Now there's a word I can live with.
I start the car and watch her
waddle away in her tight blue shorts.

Mantis

     (... he suffered a loss of proprioception ...)

Hand rolls down window of Chevrolet.
Eyes stare at lawn gone wild.
Remember mowing many times,
years ago. Sometimes got down on knees,
pulled back blades, studied
how they moved, insects. Some quick,
always busy. Some slow, leg suspended
in mid-air, mid stride.

Why won't she come and drive?
Wonder why was sent back here
since she cannot bear to touch,
cannot tolerate sound of reconstructed
voice. Look at hand, command it
to aim and wave at neighbors rolling out
trash or strolling with kids.

Children grown now, strangers
since time woke up one morning
and did not know arms, or feet,
or any other part of body
that stretched out on sheets and held
thoughts loosely like palsied hand.
Michael James Robertson, man, something
that had always been. Discovered
could make body move if whipped like ox.

Disguised as old something in mirror,
though usual smile could not be found
among twinges of unwilling muscles.

She called in sick. Sent kids to stay
with neighbors,
                      while tried to make body
tighten down against true intentions,
or failing that, cause thinking to fill
and swell against inner edges.
Night, prayed to god of deep sleep,
god of change for no good reason,
to bring soul and flesh together again
like old friends—

make them embrace, shake hands, agree.
Today, wait on passenger side.
Years now since sat behind web
of wheel, held cold keys in fingers
and felt engine shudder to start.
Hands float in space around head,
wave at her face in bedroom window.
She's staring at
like she did all morning
as crept over lawn toward car,
having to capture each foot with
eyes as always, lifting it, moving it
through air, letting it drop to ground....

Is she looking at dark clouds
beyond distant buildings? Does she
think about thin body
stalking her with patience
in dim light of silent room? She
who put on smiling mask and never
took it off.
                Just want her to drive to
city, where great blades of buildings
flash above, where body waits
inside each posture, for ones who shove
against wall with fierceness that makes
feel myself again right out to edges,
right out to places where something old
can end.

The Men

Campbell's legs are long and straight
like the great blue heron's,
and his giant wing tip shoes
sweep low over the ground,
the plastic ends of his laces
whipping around like horse-flies.
His hat brushes among leaves
snapping off limbs like bean pods
and popping an occasional power line.
Sometimes his long freckled hands
appear around corners, as if
they had eyes themselves.
He was elected mayor many years ago
in the last days of women
and has remained in office
by acclamation ever since.
His eyes can be seen
way up there
moving in their sockets
like the eyes of a hawk
surveying the world of small things below.

Jennings has large birds
for hands. Crows, some say.
When he walks by
they light on the backs of chairs,
the rims of lamp shades,
the heads of boys,
the statues of women,

and have to be dragged away.
Sometimes they light
on his own shoulders
and exhausted
he lets them stay there,
preening themselves,
chirping softly into his ears.
But what a squawking racket they make
when he forces them into pockets
or to perch on a handle of any kind.
Sometimes they curl up against his belly
one on top of the other
and sleep.
Then his own eyes close
and a smile
creeps into his face.

Goodwin has stakes instead of feet.
He can walk
but it's slow going
the way he struggles
to draw each step from the ground.
Mostly he stays put
just passing the time of day.
He knows the best locations:
in front of Burns's store,
or along the main path in the park.
He's good at giving directions
if you are new in town

or lost or drunk.
Sometimes his eyes grow dark,
he weeps like a child
who's seen more than he should.
But then the customers feel guilty
and shy away,
or the boys in the park
are frightened by his eyes,
by his hands that want to grab them
as they run by
so he can hold them still and explain.
The police come and pull him up,
carry him off and plant him
at the edge of town
with a warning to move on.
But he always comes back,
determinedly happy at first,
tipping his hat,
speaking to everyone,
always ready with an answer
to any question.

Bailey left here
large as a mountain
in the days of women
and returned gaunt
two years later
after they'd gone.
He still carries the old belt with him,

six inches wide
with a great silver buckle.
Holding it in both hands
like a woman lifting her hem,
he walks within its circle.
If someone avoids him
he loops it over their shoulders
and pulls them close.
Then they listen
or pretend to, at least,
trying to avoid his unblinking stare
and the sharp pulse of his breath
till he raises the belt and lets them go.
Sometimes he grows tired of that belt,
throws it over his shoulder
like a huge strap attached to nothing,
or lets it drop on the ground around his feet,
kicking it before him like a dead limb,
leaving its track of overlapping circles.

Only Walker still remembers
some of the women
in particular and by name.
Natalie was his wife
who bore him a daughter, Jean,
and two sons: Franklin
for the famous Ben, and Joshua
because it sounded good.
Only the boys are with him now.

There haven't been women here
for years, except for statues
with birds on their shoulders
and missing arms. He says
it was like a parade, the women
walking hand in hand in the street
till they disappeared at the edge of town
like a herd of white-tailed deer
strolling into woods at dusk.
Staked out at the town limits
after another bout of sadness,
Goodwin waved his handkerchief and wept.
Hugo claims to remember too,
says the women were evil plotters,
better gone to some other place.
But the men lean toward Walker's view
because he's given up all work,
just sits on his porch
waiting for someone
to stop and ask.

The Man in the Green Truck

I stood at the edge of starlight
and the darkness of thick trees,
leaned on a small maple that bent
to hold me. Sweating, itching
from the scrape of bark and leaves,
I couldn't see or hear the small
green truck as it bounced
over the dirt road just beyond
the rise of the hill, headlights
rippling through pines and over
tombstones, the cinderblock church
where three men wearing camouflage
gathered to drink, guns lounging
on the hoods of their cars. The light
of that truck must have swept over
the x'ed doors of the barn where geldings
stood still as the trees outside
their stalls, and into the tall windows
of my friend's house, playing over
the conversation pit and the dark fireplace
loaded with artificial logs. Nearby, I was
the one who didn't hear the screams
of my neighbor trying to walk off
the stress of a day's work when a man
dragged her into the woods and beat her
to death, stealing her clothes and a ring.
I walked through those woods proud
of the nervous edge that made me alert,
one hand a shield against spiderwebs,

the other fending off branches of scrub-oak.
I crossed the dirt road, then picked my way
through the thicket beside the church,
whistling to warn any armed drunks
that I am only a man, not a doe.
I crossed the hardtop and entered the gate
of my chain-link fence, the silence
of dogs who know me only too well.
My wife was safe and already asleep.
Next day, I was questioned by police
who said my face was like the one
described by neighbors. But they knew
I wasn't the man in the green truck.
Instead, I am the man
who stood at the edge of woods
observing the spread of moonlight
on a field, absorbing the sounds
of the night behind me: cicadas,
tree frogs, chuck-will's-widows,
the human sounding steps of deer
among leaves... and practiced
meditation, a technique that dissolves
each thought as it arises, each dream,
desire and fear.

The Chair

Returning to the box
of sweet dry cereal,
he glances into shade
beyond the kitchen window:
Someone's brought a chair
and left it on the porch.
He finds the back door key,
carefully steps down
to the gray, warped boards
of the porch floor
crosshatched with pinestraw
and dry brown leaves:
thick square legs,
seat and back not curved
to cup the body's shape.
It isn't old, but new,
the wood unfinished, yellow,
still full of juice,
heavy as the dead weight
of Sam the black lab, the day
he carried him to his grave
beside the house. He looks
around, but no one's hiding
in the broken-down Ford,
no one laughing to himself
behind the metal shed,
door swung open on darkness.
He goes inside and gets
the broom—short, quick strokes

following the cracks
between boards, dry bristles
breaking as he bends
to reach under the chair.
Out of breath, he discovers
the seat and back are shaped
after all, settling around him
like the bones and flesh of a hand.
Good work, he thinks
and takes a deep breath, surveying
his small kingdom swollen
by the year's unhampered grass
and weeds. The broom leans now
against the rail. You can stay
for a while can't you, the man
asks his thin friend.
The answer—a shuffling
under leaves, the overgrown fields
nodding within themselves,
the distant arch of woods,
the cool mist that slowly
overtakes it all.

Not Talking at Dawn

He stands in the mouth of his garage
with a pine board in his hands.
Morning light etches the details
of his neighbor's porch rail and shutters
and the white mortar between bricks,
the sublunar landscape of pine bark
awaking to the traffic of ants and lizards
and those small jumping spiders with big eyes.
He rises early in order to get more done
and he would say something about that
but getting more done is only yesterday's dream,
and no one is listening. He sands a board
and applies the first coat for another
shelf in the basement, loving the smell
of that dark walnut stain. He feels
a familiar stillness burning into the slow
unfolding of his nerves, into the long
loosening of his joints like the way the stain
heightens the fluid grain of this common pine,
feels the steady adhesion of his jaw, teeth
settling into their perfect fit.
As he lays the board in its place—
he will drive the nails tomorrow—
he wonders what teeth and bones
would have to say if left to themselves.
He remembers the skull his science teacher
brought into class years ago, turning it carefully
so everyone could see, pointing out
the parietal, occipital and temporal bones,

probing the foramen magnum with two fingers.
He remembers the heft of it in his own hands,
how awake it seemed without flesh,
without tongue or voice.

The Crawl

His father broke his face when he was five.
He sits in the bus station and tries to grin
at passersby, settles in and reads the paper.
For years he guarded J. C. Penney's. He
strolled from lingerie to men's suits, flashed

his light on the alabaster arms of manniquins.
By three he slipped away to the bar across
the street, maintained visual contact,
bought another Johnny Walker Red for Shirley.
"You're the craziest man I know," she said,

then left with some guy in boots and blazer.
He lost that job when Penney's moved to the mall.
His mother died and the house grew big as Texas.
He studies departures and arrivals, bends
the paper so he can see beyond the words.

On Saturdays when the weather's good
he shows up at the lake with Shirley.
They strip and wade into the water.
"His face is a squashed banana," whispers
a hidden boy, laughing. "No," says the girl,

"a dead squirrel complete with whiskers."
Shirley floats on her back like a small island.
The ugliest man in town does the slowest
crawl she's ever seen, his hands dropping
all around her body like tiny parachutes.

Let Me Find It

The Other

When you fell behind
I refused to see
because it wasn't true,
only a dream of yours
trying the body on for size.

Later when you took the lead,
dropping down bright-eyed and rested
from overhanging limbs
just when I thought I was alone,
I didn't alter my pace
but kept it steady,
knowing that you would grow tired
and we would meet again.

At first your tracks
were dark impressions on damp grass
and I planted mine beside them
like the matching halves of shells,
but then the days wore on
and your prints became as faint
as the breath of stones,
and I found myself stopping to rest
more often
in the homes of kind strangers.

I let the sun rise in windows.
I let the sleep drain slowly out of my eyes.
I let the voices of children settle over me

like falling leaves.
I let the mistress' housecat curl up at my feet.
Sometimes I stayed for weeks
letting the minutes come to me one at a time
like surprised birds out of a great vastness,
forgetting the wasted work of centuries
and the plodding cattle of expectation.

One day I stayed forever
and nobody seemed to mind.
I was a friend of the family,
better than no trouble at all.
I was a grandfather who had died
many years ago in another country
come back to life.
I worked in the yard
and made wise mutterings to the children
about the palaces of princes
and the death-smells of prison.
I lived in my own rooms
among the slow accumulation of books.

One day you appeared at the door
wearing the mask of your old man's face,
and nobody objected at first
that I wanted you to stay.
I embraced you like my own true brother.
I brought you fresh clothes.
I brought food made especially for you.

I let your sleep fall deeply into morning,
the sun drawing out the pain of your exhaustion
through open windows.
We sat together on the back porch
gazing into the depths of trees,
letting the tight threads of our voices
unwind in great piles of equal size
at our feet.
You brought me your tales of the terrors.
You brought me your love of the work undone.
You brought me the vision of a young girl
with the voice of a recurring dream
and the body of God.

One day my family said
times are too hard
for two worthless grandfathers
in the same house.
We took to the road together

happy with each direction that called us,
our words like fresh vegetables and fruits,
holding nothing in our pockets
that had not been given
by the other.

The Motel

His hand on the nozzle and his upturned face
ripple in the rising fumes of gas.
We ask him about the land and weather.
He says it ain't exactly cool here in the summer
or warm in the winter either,
invites us to settle down
and even offers me a job.

Gas spurts from the tank
and drains down the side of our car.
We pay him what we owe him
but he keeps on smiling and talking
and looking out past us
at something we cannot see
swimming in the air.

My wife and I drive into town
to have a look around: a few
old buildings strung out, sand-blasted houses,
a store, couple of pickups, gas station,
skinny dog pacing outside a door,
tumbleweeds trapped against abandoned cars,
and the tortured carpet of the prairie rolling out.

If more than fifty people live here
they are living underground.
Tornadoes threaten,
crosswinds spring
from the shallow mouths of gulches.

There is nothing here and no one here,
and yet. . . .

We turn around and hit the freeway
and drive a hundred miles into darkness.
Suddenly, thousands of lights
before us as far as we can see
like the spirit of one of those old herds of buffalo
holding to the land. But there is
nothing spiritual about it.

A hot bath, a hot dinner, a hot temper,
broken glass and a fat alley cat,
a couple of stiff ones in the lounge,
the comforting smell of lysol,
a double bed wide as a prairie
and a television deep as the wind
finally bring us back to the only sense we have.

One by One

The world was full of animals.
The yellow cat swaggered,
pressed his face into mine,
needle-point teeth grazing my cheek,

cold breath reeking of mouse-blood.
The loner ticks lived deep in his fur,
heads buried safely in flakey skin,
gray bodies fattening under the summer moon.

He trotted into the woods one day,
ears pricked, tail straightened,
and never came back. Then there was
the bow-legged boxer who caught me

by the folded cuff of my jeans
and dragged me around the yard
till Mother came running to save me.
He bounded along the fence

just laughing and cavorting,
then knocked me down again
and licked my face. He never
recovered from his two back legs

broken by a car. The vet's needle
drew the breath out of him
and made his eyes go blank.
One day a Black Snake longer than I was

when stretched out beside it
escaped from the drainage ditch
into the transplanted Spruce
and White Pine of the front yard

and had to be killed
with a pitch-fork and a .22.
Its skin shone and glinted for a week
on my neighbor's chain link fence.

The small green parakeet
stepped from my sister's finger
to perch on the ridge of her teeth,
turning to cock his head and stare

into the curved cavern of her breath,
but still he never said a word
that wasn't his own.
And no word at all

when he was caught
by the cat, bulging from its mouth
like a colorful egg, still alive,
eyes even calmer than usual.

Opening Night

The lights go down
and the curtain rises.
I pour a glass of wine
but you don't enter.
I keep on cooking dinner,
looking for you in the shadows
of stage left.
I pour another glass of wine
and wave it in the air,
but still you don't
storm through the door,
throw your purse at the couch.
André whispers from the wings,
telling me not to panic.
The audience is amused,
discussing the half empty bottle of wine
that symbolizes life's incompleteness,
the amorphous stuffed animal on the couch
that hints at an uncertain love,
but how long can their indulgence last?
André, thin, quick as a reflection,
holds the cast together backstage
with vague promises.
He will get this show on the road
and collect his reviews if it kills him.
I bring our dinner to the table,
slide your plate before the empty chair:
baked chicken over rice, green beans.
I eat mine first, then yours.

I fall asleep in my chair
and dream of long hours at the shore
lying flat on my back,
line of frigate birds in the sky above me
like a disembodied spine.
Weeks have passed, and the audience
grows tired and hungry.
Blankets have been brought in,
emergency food and nurses.
Tonight we serve soup and cheese sandwiches.
I can feel a sickness coming on from watching
André die in the wings like a fish
trapped in a shallow pool on the beach,
or is it me that's dying?
The critics left days ago,
handkerchiefs pressed to their faces,
but return on occasion to see how it's going.
So far, if I can read their eyes correctly
from this distance, I think
I've been favorably received,
but one never knows
until the morning after opening night.
Maybe then I'll wake to that
required stab of anguish in my belly,
your silhouette in the doorway
on cue for a change,
newspaper tucked neatly
under your arm.

Something

I knew
why my sons and daughters would never be
born, never take to the field or the dance floor,
never stand beside my hospital bed

sad and full of confessions
they're afraid to make.
I understood completely my mother's fear of deep
water, her love of bright colors,

music that thumps and laughs,
easy puzzles, games of chance.
My secret theories explained
why my father's bones manufactured rogue cells

that ate his blood, consumed him
from the inside out, a man who quit school
to deliver groceries, who carried the coal
home to a small fire every night

in the long winter of 1934.
Lying on his bed before the coma, he told me
how clear it all becomes
when there is no future and the past

grows stale. He remembered how he
carried that coal bucket in the crook of his arm
across the room where his father
slumped in the big chair wondering how he'd managed

to lose it all: business, property, savings.
I knew everything once.
Explanations climbed out of me
like circus clowns from a tiny car. But after

all these years I still can't explain
that message in my father's face
the day before he slipped into the hole
inside himself—a sleep he broke from only

minutes before he died, lucid, wanting to pray,
only the night nurse at hand—
the hint of a smile, something
waiting for him beyond the body of pain.

A Drawing of the Laughing Jesus

Beside my window
looking out on pine trees,
Jesus throws his head back
and laughs out loud, and the air
which once held his famous body
continues to expand molecule
by molecule over the face
of the earth.
A believing friend of mine
gave me the laughing Jesus
many years ago at a time
when I was striking the word *Lord*
and all it means
from my heart.
Since then, at the price
of my faith, I have wandered
among the possibilities, flicking
on the light of each room,
sticking my head in for a quick view.
The answers raise their slow heads
from the sleep of centuries
and stare until I leave.
I keep the drawing of Jesus
for the way he laughs
with his mouth gaping open
like a drunk, for the ordinary light
of afternoon reflecting off his face,
for the effeminate cock of his wrist
as he holds his hand to his chest.

I like to forget his name, to imagine
the hoarse crack of his laugh, the air
around him ripe with the smell of sweat
and wine, to believe this was a man
who watched each fear
as it rose on the horizon
and laughed it out of mind and body forever.

Paid Vacation

In the long hours you lie among your furniture
counting breaths and watching light fall
into corners. What will you do
at seven in the morning when the clock
holds its peace? Discover the trees
in the back yard, or catch up on
the worries that are waiting for you
in this sudden silence? Have all
your bills been paid? What about
the weeds taking over your yard?
Where does the labor of this constant
maintaining end, and real time begin?

Maybe there's departure
when a red-faced man in a baseball cap
sneaks up behind you like a Hollywood Indian
raising universal gestures above your head,
or when your daughter finds you over the manhole
staring into darkness, or when your son
finds you racking up the balls
in a dark room stained with light and smoke,
or when your woman finds you
climbing to the core of an old volcano
to watch the sun sink its razor teeth
into cold stone.

Go ahead and let the world you've made
return to dust. Let the past return to weeds
and lovely, indistinguishable trees.

Then maybe there can be those hours
when the blade of your eyes softens into light,
when the stone of your hurled voice
breaks open into flowers
falling on the heads of children.
Then maybe that moment will come
when a red-faced man in a baseball cap
sneaks up behind you with a gun
like the spirit of some hard ancestral thief
who has come into this time of awkward emptiness
to take you for everything
you're worth.

Finesse

when it seems as though the days
are made of white paper
that the blue and white afghan
tossed over the back of the chair
will drape in that disheveled way forever
while the brown leaves outside
continue to twitch in their sleep
still attached still resisting the wind
with dreams of a draught
from so deep in the earth
the flavor is of stone and fossil

when the trees facing in all directions
turn into light
like the flash of a million spoons
and the sound of a black snake in the grass
can be heard only with eyes closed
under the multiple songs
of the mocking bird

then suddenly the voices of young men
will slice over the blacktop over the lawns
the deep bass of their music
shuttering in the panes of glass
and in your hands
which have grown numb
in the first cold air from the west

and you will stand in your own yard
staring through that curtain of trees
that no longer hides the neighbors' windows
a view of their vague movements
gray smoke pouring from chimneys

you will turn and look into your dog's eyes
he obeys only you
drops the soggy ball at your feet
and for one moment
nothing else matters
the distance you throw it
the rightness of the bounce

The Messengers

Two young ones appear at my door,
sun going down behind them.
They don't care that it's cold,
that the way home is long.
Pushing past me, smiling, benevolent,
they sit in unison on the couch,
clothes identical and neat,
faces clean and rosy.
Later, you will thank us, they say,
but you may begin by serving us.
So I bring them roast duck and wine:
your duck is too cold, says one,
your wine is too warm, says the other,
but there is no promise of pleasure.
So I bring them my eyes on a platter,
my ears between slices of bread:
your eyes are as full as the loggers' stream,
they say, eating them like olives,
your ears do an injustice to this fine bread,
and they eat them like Canadian bacon,
stuffing the bread into pockets.
So I bring them my heart at the end of a sword,
and they inspect it, laughing,
tossing it back and forth,
testing the degree of their skills,
behind the back, under the leg, knuckleball.
There is only so much we can do, they say,
dropping the thing in an ashtray,
straightening their narrow black ties.

It's a gracious plenty, I say.
At a pre-arranged signal they stand,
they step to the door and I follow,
they linger outside,
I pull the door to a crack.
Thank the Lord for what you've received, they say,
voices going up in cold smoke,
and I shut the door saying thank you
Thank you.

Privacy

Some of the ones who were still dry
edged toward the pond, removing their
watches. They wanted to be chased
and caught, carried and thrown, wanted
the sudden cold plunge not of their
choosing, the collapse of water over their

heads. Some of them ran into the barn
and hid, hunkered down in a stall beneath
a gelding's bulk—the clunk of hooves,
curious lips nibbling their hair—and still
we found them, flushed them out into
the night air shrieking like surprised birds.

You I chased into the storage shed.
You laughed and danced like a child
side-hopping the wheelbarrow's handles,
grazing the shanks of the long-faced
shovels, the tractor's blue motor still
ticking. I chased you over the path
between paddocks where old mares
lay in the grass, mesmerized by the full moon.

I chased you back to the crowded pond,
still breathing hard. *What took you so
long*, you said. You fended me off with slaps
and kicks, hands quick as fish protecting
their beds. But I grabbed you and picked you
up and carried you mock-screaming to the water's

edge. The water clapped shut above us,
the cold rang through us, we held each other
all the way down, the only sound our breaths
bundled and carried away.

The Guest

Thanks for stopping by
thanks for bringing all of the roses
and the fingernail clippings
just what I needed
thanks for saying the right things
about beauty and grace and the new millenium
and how the food won't go to waste
and the trees will grow ten times as fast
and there's nothing to worry about
thanks for dropping in unannounced
my underwear are clean enough
and what is there to hide anyway
nothing you haven't seen before
in one form or another
and besides I do not need my sleep
not like some who are working
two jobs or three and have kids
and many thanks for those disparaging remarks
I needed a good pep talk
I will pour out my gin
I will strangle the cat that evil dirty thing
with my bare hands
and toss her in the dumpster
and I'll bear the scars of that small battle
in remembrance of this fond visit
unannounced as a gust of wind
and thanks too for leaving the door open
and for throwing open all the windows
I need more light more air no doubt about that

I need the birds in my hair
now that the cat is defunct
and beetles scramble over the floor's rough terrain
so thank you my dear friend
I make a gift to you of my gnarly chest hair
my navel lint my toes salute you
I shall bring out the cheese and saltines
and two glasses for the wine you bought
but forgot to bring

Before Daylight

A car passes close in the pre-dawn.
My mind feels as old as the moon,
as old as the spider-light of stars.
I walk out into late summer air.
Early-risers lean against their cars
waiting for some small fire
to crack in their brains.
The road shoulders off into perfect grass.
The air is framed with wires,
the houses still and dark.
I follow my dog
into the strip of wild growth
under the power line,
the inkling of a path
like a deer trail's faint disturbance of leaves.
It slips among giant weeds
and poles that hum with vigilance overhead.
It runs behind Prather's Car and Truck Repair,
then over the tracks,
moon blazing on the rails,
then behind the new restaurant
that serves American and Chinese,
behind Buddy Coleman's Hardware,
cardboard boxes on the loading dock
collecting dust and rain,
behind the VFW no. 5932,
the silent playground of the middle school,
the small brown and gray houses
where the cats crouch down and stare.

My dog is onto something,
this mindless running under the wires
into the cool mist clinging to pastures,
the sleeping herd spiraling
like a dark galaxy on the yellow slope,
then into the cold low darkness of woods
where owls and whippoorwills
warn the hillsides ahead,
the underbrush whipping my skin to blood,
my body blasting the spiders
from the long night of their webs.
It is still dark
and I can run without effort
learning to lope like my golden dog
who finds nothing to retrieve.

Uncle

The water grew high on the wall.
My castles had long since fallen,
washed away.

Then came to the top of the wall
the man I called Uncle,
sent by my father to find me,
railroad man with the engineer's cap,
work-naked-in-the-yard man,
hunting and fishing man,

so I ran away through the knee-deep water
not ready to give up my games,
nipples salt-sore in the wind,
legs burning from the long day of sun,
and ignored the old man's voice
calling my name.

But then my foot reaching out
found nothing but water,
my face was slapped shut by water,
my hands, held high above my head
like visible screams, fell
from the edge of air into water.
Three times I tried to climb out
but the sand gave way like smoke,
gave way like the world to a child
gone suddenly blind, deaf and dumb.

Till finally I just lay there
giving up to the god of my Sunday school,
giving up to the god of salt water and fish
my life which was not so far on its way
that it couldn't be taken back again
like a bad move in a friendly game of chess.

And when I gave up,
I rose from the bottom,
air splashed my face,
seagulls were squealing,
and Uncle stood at the top of the wall—
hair white on his chest,
old eyes squinting in the sun,
looking out beyond me,
calling me home.

Let Me Find It

Let me find it today, in the aftermath
of the crow's call from the tall pine
outside my window, in the flickering

of dry leaves still caught in the limbs
among buds, in the cat's sinking back
into haunches, poised, some sense

of how the body should proceed on this day
when the clouds accumulate like one great
wave off shore. Something

slow to build, smooth in its entry
like a breeze in a tunnel where a child hides
in his niche to watch cars, to listen

for the long ascension of their coming on,
the flickering play of lights on the rough cut
of stone, the sudden flash of bottled faces,

the rattle of debris against rock walls,
the falling away of sound like the breath
going out slowly for a long time. Let me

find it this time knowing that it will do
no good, that it's only the ground under
my feet, the sound of my own words

returning like the radar of bats. Knowing
that it's only this movement of my hands
toward the bare waist of the woman

brushing her hair at the dresser, only the long
line of my eye casting over and over
into the streets and rooms, too fed-up with

waiting ever to be patient again. Let me
find it again today as I have before
among trees and fields, knowing that it's

only the rise of one moment against all others,
a bursting into flame, and then the flame,
and then the wind that carries it away.

Biographical Note

Jim Peterson is a poet, novelist, and playwright. His recent books have been published by Red Hen Press: *The Owning Stone* (poetry, 2000, 2011, winner of The Benjamin Saltman Award), *Paper Crown* (novel, 2005), and *The Bob and Weave* (poetry, 2006). Other poetry collections include *The Man Who Grew Silent* (The Bench Press, 1989), *Carvings on a Prayer Tree* (Holocene Press, a chapbook, 1994), *An Afternoon With K* (Holocene Press, 1996), and *Jim Peterson's Greatest Hits 1984-2000* (Pudding House, 2000, 2003). His poems have appeared in such journals as *Poetry*, *Georgia Review*, *Prairie Schooner*, *Shenandoah*, *Poetry Northwest*, *Texas Review*, *Connecticut Review*, etc. His plays have been produced in regional and college theatres. He and his wife have traveled in Peru studying Andean shamanic culture. When not writing or teaching, he enjoys riding his motorcycle around the country and hiking in its mountains, deserts, river canyons, and high plains. He is on the faculty of the University of Nebraska's Low-Residency MFA Program in Creative Writing and is Writer in Residence and Coordinator of Creative Writing at Randolph College in Lynchburg, Virginia where he lives with his wife Harriet and their beloved Welsh Corgis, Dylan Thomas and Mama Kilya.